Pure Blind Faith Guidebook

"Your Gift of Faith"
by
Lisa Willice Silva

Table of Content

Chapter 1   Getting Ready   page 3
Chapter 2   GOD'S Words of Faith   page 5
Chapter 3   What is Faith?   page 7
Chapter 4   Quotes of faith   page 14
Chapter 5   Blind Faith   page 18
Chapter 6   Visual Faith   page 20
Chapter 7   Envy and Jealous   page 24
Chapter 8   Personalize your Faith   page 28
Chapter 9   Money, Fame & Happiness   page 30
Chapter 10   Love   page 32
Chapter 11   Imagine your Faith   page 39
Chapter 12   GOD's Timing   page 45
Chapter 13   Remember   page 53

Chapter One
Getting Ready

For this guidebook you will need a pen or pencil. You will be asked questions that you can answer in length within the book, a journal or a notebook.

I wrote this study guidebook to go along with my book. "Pure Blind Faith." on Amazon, Kindle or iPad.

Though you can enjoy the guidebook without the "Pure Blind Faith" book. Its even more powerful with it.

When you see this symbol its referring to the book Pure Blind Faith (PBF). It will follow up with the chapter and page number. It will look like this (PBF Ch 0, Pg 0)

My prayer for you is to naturally develop this special gift that God gave us all.

With that said, lets start this journey.

Pure Blind Faith

How would you define the word *faith*? (write it down)

Chapter Two
God's Words of Faith:

"Because you have so little faith. I tell you the truth, if you have faith as small as a mustard seed, you can say to this mountain, 'Move from here to there' and it will move. Nothing will be impossible for you."
Matthew 17:20 (NIV)

"If you have faith as small as a mustard seed, you can say to this mulberry tree, 'Be uprooted and planted in the sea,' and it will obey you.
Luke 17:6 (NIV)

This is what GOD has asked of us, to have **faith** as small as a mustard seed. A crumb!

This is my story on how it started. (PBF Ch 1, Pg 4-8)

Pure Blind Faith

What does God's word about *Faith* mean to you?
(write it down)

Chapter Three
What is *faith*?

The encyclopedia defines it as:

Faith is confidence or trust in a person, thing, super-natural being, or in the doctrines or teachings of a religion. It is also belief that is not based on proof.

In religion, **faith** often involves accepting claims about the character of a super-natural, nature, or the universe. While some have argued that **faith** is opposed to reason, proponents of faith argue that the proper domain of **faith** concerns questions which cannot be settled by evidence. For example, **faith** can be applied to predictions of the future, which (by definition) has not yet occurred. The word **faith** is often used as a substitute for hope, trust, a dream, wish or belief.

The dictionary defines it as:

Something that is believed especially with strong conviction; especially: a system of religious beliefs.

Loyalty to duty or a person

Keeping a promise or sincerity of intentions.

Belief and trust in and loyalty to God: belief in the traditional doctrine of a religion.

Firm belief in something for which there is no proof: Complete trust.

The Thesaurus defines it as:

- acceptance
- belief
- confidence
- conviction
- hope
- loyalty
- truth
- allegiance
- assent
- assurance
- certainty
- certitude
- constance
- credit

Man's definition of faith:

aggressiveness
arrogance
assuredness
audacity
boldness
bravery
certainty
certitude
conviction
coolness
courage
firmness
nerve
poise
positiveness
presumption
security
self-confidence
self-reliance
sureness
surety
temerity
trust

Things I heard:

When referring to my pure blind faith, I was told these things:

*I was crazy enough to think everything I pray for will happen.

*I lived in a fantasy world.

*Wake up Lisa, this is the real world. Things don't happen like that.

*I was a dreamer.

*How will you do that without money?

*You can't afford it?

Once I made a paper doll picture of my family. I had just given birth to my daughter, Soleil Love (PBF Ch 14, Pg 93-96) Though in the picture was a father, mother, little girl holding a doll and a baby boy. My mother saw the picture and said, "Who's the little boy?" I said, 'Our son Ocean." She said, "You're pregnant, you just had Soleil?"

I wasn't pregnant though that's how I visualized my family. She said, "What if you have another girl?" I said, "I won't mom, the next baby will be our son Ocean." I figured Soleil would be around 2 years old when Ocean is born. That's why she was holding a doll in the picture. Well, my faith came true. Soleil was 2 1/2 when Ocean Peace was born. (PBF Ch 14, Pg 98-103)

Faith terms:

His supporters have accepted his claims with blind **faith**.

Our **faith** in the government has been badly shaken by the recent scandals.

Lending him the money to start his own business was an act of **faith.**

It requires a giant leap of **faith** for us to believe that she is telling the truth.

Nothing is more important to her than her **faith** in God.

She says that her *faith* has given her courage to deal with this tragedy.

Without question I took everything he said on *faith.*

Even in the movie Star Wars Episode IV, Darth Vader (delivered by James Earl Jones) recited this line…

"I find your lack of *faith* disturbing"

"I have *faith* in you my son."

That surely defines what God feels about our lack of *faith*.

Pure Blind Faith

Do you know any faith quotes?(write it down)

Chapter Four
Quotes of Faith

"Be *faithful* in small things because it is in them that your strength lies."
Mother Teresa

"*Faith* is taking the first step even when you don't see the whole staircase."
Martin Luther King, Jr.

"*Faith* is the strength by which a shattered world shall emerge into the light."
Helen Keller

"If patience is worth anything, it must endure to the end of time. And a living *faith* will last in the midst of the blackest storm."   Gandhi

"*Faith* activates God - Fear activates the Enemy."
Joel Osteen

"*Faith* and prayer are the vitamins of the soul; man cannot live in health without them."
Mahalia Jackson

"Sometimes life hits you in the head with a brick. Don't lose *faith*."   Steve Jobs

"The way to see by *faith* is to shut the Eye of Reason."
                                        Benjamin Franklin

"My family, frankly, they weren't folks who went to church every week. My mother was one of the most spiritual people I knew but she didn't raise me in the church, so I came to my Christian *faith* later in life and it was because the precepts of Jesus Christ spoke to me in terms of the kind of life that I would want to lead."
                                        Barack Obama

"Always be yourself, express yourself, have *faith* in yourself, do not go out and look for a successful personality and duplicate it."
                                        Bruce Lee

"Scientists were rated as great heretics by the church, but they were truly religious men because of their *faith* in the orderliness of the universe."
                                        Albert Einstein

"Resist your fear; fear will never lead to you a positive end. Go for your **faith** and what you believe." T. D. Jakes

"I have come to the conclusion that the most important element in human life is **faith**."
Rose Kennedy

Prayer never loses its reward. Prayer is the key to the kingdom and **Faith** unlocks the door.
Rev, Douglas Goggins Jr. (My father)

Faith is canceling out fear and living your life victoriously.
Daryl C. Silva aka The Boston Dad (my husband)

My personal quote:

"Nothing changed around us, but everything changed within us. Through love and **faith** GOD renewed our marriage, our walk, our love and our family's path."
Lisa Willice Goggins Silva

What would be your own personal quote of faith?
(write it down)

Chapter Five
Blind Faith

Name things you have done in faith, belief or trust, just because you felt it was going to happen or that things would be okay? Something you bought, sold or just tried, not knowing it would come to pass or knowing the outcome.

Here's a few from the book…
(PBF CH 2, Pg 9-14)   (PBF CH 3, Pg 16-17)
(PBF CH 10, Pg 60-62)

Samples of this:
Putting a down payment on something promising in your life (house, ring, car) knowing you will get the balance and be able to buy this item.

Going out for dinner with friends without money, praying somehow it will be covered. Then when you get to the restaurant, your friends utter the words, "My treat, you paid last time."

Even putting something on layaway is an act of faith. You're believing you're going to get the merchandise out before the due date.

Pure Blind Faith

\What have you done in Faith? (write it down)

Chapter Six
Visual Faith

Have you ever had visual faith? Like cutting pictures of things you liked, an outfit, shoes, a color or design of a room, a car you desire, your dream home, a pet you would like to own, an island you would like to visit, or your dream vacation?

When you're buying paint for a room, you can visualize what the room will look like after you paint it, that's a form of faith. Sometimes it doesn't look the way your saw it. Sometimes God doesn't see it the same way you do.

Once my husband and I painted a room a creamy tan color, it looked dull. It wasn't as vibrant on the wall as the paint store sample made it look. When we painted the next room, we decided to prime it first, give it a clean slate, then paint it. It came out vibrant and the color popped out of the wall. It was so beautiful. Needless to say, we went back to the first room, primed it and repainted it. That's what God wants us to do, start with a clean slate. So we can be vibrant for HIM.

We have Pinterest to keep folders of things you like or projects you like to do in the future. Though before Pinterest, when I was living on a boat alone in Marina Del Rey, I would cut out pictures of things I wanted in my future like a happy family, a bigger boat & a computer. I hung these pictures on the wall, prayed over them & visualized.

Things I prayed for…..
(PBF Ch 5, Pg 23)
(PBF Ch 8, Pg 47-49)
(PBF Ch 15, Pg 130)

Well, within time, it all came true. Not the same boat, though a bigger boat, a new Apple computer & a very happy family, years later. Think back and name something you cut out of a magazine, a newspaper or a book hoping to have it one day. Something you have been thinking about, visualizing and even praying for.

A few years ago, my best friend & Floridian sister found out she was pregnant. Having had two boys already, each pregnancy she prayed it was the girl God has promised her. However, God had other plans for her. This pregnancy was going to be her last and she prayed it would be a girl, God's promise to her. I drew her a fancy name card and framed it with her daughters name on it. I told her "Pray over it & live as if your daughter is already here and God had already answered your prayer." Her husband stated, "What if it's a boy, do you have a name framed for a boys name?" "No," I said, that wouldn't be faith if I did one for a boy." I told her, "Buy only girls clothes and baby items that are pink. Talk to her in your tummy and say her name." She said she hated the color pink. I told her, "Learn to love it cause your house is going to be filled with pink." When she received the ultrasound, her prayers were confirmed, It was indeed a girl. Well she got obsessed with buying clothes, shoes and especially bows. She went crazy & took it to a whole other level. Now her house is an explosion of pink & her daughter is here with 2 amazing big brothers and I'm a proud Godmother.

Though you have not seen him, you love him; and even though you do not see him now, you believe in him and are filled with an inexpressible and glorious joy,
1 Peter 1:8

What have you done in visual faith? (write it down)

Chapter Seven
Envy and Jealousy

Remember not to envy what another person has. You may want something similar, though you don't want what they have. It wasn't meant for you, it was designed for that individual. It is the answer to Their prayer, not yours. It is the desire of their heart, not yours. Many times, it is this that leads to jealousy & envy.

Jealousy is the fear that something which we possess will be taken away by another person. Although jealousy can apply to our jobs, our possessions or our reputations, the word more often refers to anxiety which comes when we are afraid that the affections of a loved one might be lost to a rival. We fear that our mates, or perhaps our children, will be lured away by some other person whom, when compared to us, seems to be more attractive, capable and/or successful.

There is a distinction between jealousy & envy. To be envious is to want something which belongs to another person.
For jealousy arouses a husband's fury, and he

will show no mercy when he takes revenge.
Proverbs 6:34

Anger is cruel, and wrath is like a flood, but jealousy is even more dangerous.
Proverbs 27:4

A heart at peace gives life to the body, but envy rots the bones.
Proverbs 14:30

Trust in your faith

Faith is something you believe God has for you, not something already belonging to another.

Each one should test their own actions. Then they can take pride in themselves alone, without comparing themselves to someone else.
Galatians 6:4

Not too long ago, I was admiring my sister's shoes. They were a Michael Kors plain black sneaker boot. I'm not into designer things. I would care less if the dollar store made them. I just thought they were cool and comfortable looking. I expressed to her how much I liked them.

A few weeks later, for my birthday, my sister sent me a pair of those shoes. It was similar to hers but had little spikes at the side for decoration. Even though they were not the same, it was very similar and I liked them more than hers. You can want something similar or even the same but you should never want theirs.

"You shall not covet your neighbor's house, his wife or his servant, his ox or donkey or anything that belongs to your neighbor."
Exodus 20:17

Name someone or something you envy or admired at times? Who would that be? What would it be? Why? (write it down)

Chapter Eight
Personalize Your Faith

Name something you know someone has, that you wish you had or someone you wish you could be? Do you really believe God couldn't do something similar or the same for you? Something thats tailored for you and you only.

What's good for one person doesn't mean its good for you. Its like trying on a dress you admire on a hanger or on someone else though when you put it on, it just didn't hold to the admiration you once had for it. It didn't look good on you.
If Gods going to create something for you, he's going to tailor it to you and no one else.

I prayed for specific things I wanted in each nanny jobs and God answered all of them, As I received that answered pray I learned to narrow it down more specifically, define it, personalize it and learned not to pray so basic or general. (PBF Ch 5, Pg 24-30) (PBF Ch 7, Pg 40-46)

This job I didn't pray for, it just came to me. The result was different than all the other jobs.(PBF Ch 14, Pg 92-94)

Name someone or something you admire? Who would that be? What would it be? What do you admire about it or them? How can you make this envy or admiration your own? Tailor it to you.

Chapter Nine
Money, Fame and Happiness

I often heard: If I had their money, I would be happy. If I was as famous as they are, I would be happy. If I won the lottery, I would be happy.

This was my experience with money. (Ch 5, pg 26-29).

If you look at many celebrities with the combination of fame and money, it doesn't look like it brought much happiness. Many have overdosed on drugs and/or alcohol. Trying to drown out their pain. They have killed themselves leaving all that money behind. Apparently money nor fame led to happiness. When God is the center of your life, you are rich in his love and he will never leave nor forsake you. You have all the money you need. Maybe not a lump though definitely as much as needed.

For the love of money is a root of all kinds of evil. Some people, eager for money, have wandered from the faith and pierced themselves with many griefs.
*****1 Timothy 6:10 KJV ·***

Do you know someone that if they had money or fame it would not bring happiness? Someone that has had one of these things and still aren't happy. Without naming names write their story down.

Chapter Ten
Love

If you learn to love yourself, the decisions you make will be better than those if you did not love yourself. It will help you enjoy a stronger path in your walk. If you feel your worthy of God's love then your heart will open up to all God has for you. You will never doubt God's love.

You can love yourself without being conceited, though confident He made you in his likeness & tailored you, like no other.

When you have self-love, you won't settle for just anything that comes your way, you will wait on God's blessings.

I know many women that feel they need a man to feel complete. Some will take anyone, anywhere & anyhow. We all know someone like that. I'm sure you have a vision of someone in your head as we speak.

When people settle, they are not waiting patiently for the one God has appointed for them, nor the situation God illustrated for them. There's a lot of times, a women will jump into a situation because it's convenient or simply right in front of their face.

I like to talk with women in bad relationships. I always ask, "Did these men show signs in the beginning of being abusive or dysfunctional? Most women say, "Yes!"

Oprah Winfrey once said something I've learned to live by, "People show you who they are, though you don't listen, you try to change them." Well, I believe that is God's job, not yours.

LOVE YOURSELF as you want HIM to love you & it will then be easier for you to love others. How can you love HIM if you're not embracing what or whom God made you to be?

This is my story of Love.
(PBF Ch 11, Pg 70-76) (PBF Ch 12, Pg 77-86)

What can you do to love yourself more? {write it down}!

Bible Verse on Love:

1 Corinthians 13:4

Love is patient, love is kind.
It does not envy, it does not boast, it is not proud.

It does not dishonor others, it is not self-seeking, it is not easily angered, it keeps no record of wrongs.

Love does not delight in evil but rejoices with the truth. It always protects, always trusts, always hopes, always perseveres. Love never fails. But where there are prophecies, they will cease; where there are tongues, they will be stilled; where there is knowledge, it will pass away.

For we know in part and we prophesy in part, but when completeness comes, what is in part disappears. When I was a child, I talked like a child, I thought like a child, I reasoned like a child. When I became a man, I put the ways of childhood behind me.

For now we see only a reflection as in a mirror; then we shall see face to face. Now I know in part; then I shall know fully, even as I am fully known. And now these three remain: faith, hope and love. But the greatest of these is love.

How can you love others or that special someone if you're not loving and respecting yourself first.

I always say if you can enjoy a movie with a nice dinner and popcorn alone then you are enjoying your own company.

If you can go to a fancy restaurant alone (not on the phone) and sit with a view in peace. Then you are loving on yourself.

My brother Derek, for the last 4 years, starts his year off with a cruise alone. At first he questioned his decision to take a cruise by himself but have learned to enjoy his own company and love himself. That would have been unheard of many years ago. I don't think he would have ever gotten on a cruise ship by himself but now he looks forward to it as a Christmas gift each year. If he didn't get it, I think he would buy it himself every

January. He is now loving his own company after being a blessing to everyone else.

1. If I speak in the tongues of men or of angels, but do not have love, I am only a resounding gong or a clanging cymbal. 2. If I have the gift of prophecy and can fathom all mysteries and all knowledge, and if I have a faith that can move mountains, but do not have love, I am nothing. 3. If I give all I possess to the poor and give over my body to hardships that I may boast, but do not have love, I gain nothing.

1 Corinthians 13:1-3

Ask yourself:

Do I love myself? Am I ready for Jesus's love? Am I ready for that special someone? Am I asking for something I can't handle?

What do you love about yourself? When God created you, what made you different from others?(write it down)

Chapter Eleven
Imagine your Faith

Can you see yourself with your object of faith? It doesn't always mean material things. It could be your health, weight loss, to find you're missing ring, or even pass a test.

Can you see yourself losing that weight? God healing that disease? Living that dream vacation? What your future husband looks like? Your future children?

One day I was frustrated after coming home from a baseball game. The stadium it was held in sat over 50,000 people. I had, at that time, been alone a long time. There, I asked God, "With all these people in this stadium, thousands, there's not one man, not one person here for me? That day I went home, opened my wallet & threw all the photos inside of it on the floor. I asked God, "Is the guy you have for me in my wallet?

Do I already know him? What's his name? Do I already know his name? What is he doing today? After looking at all the pictures laying on the floor of different kids in my life, kids with their parents, kids school pictures, kids with me & kids with Santa, I thought, "Wow, I know you have someone out there for me, though he's obviously not in my wallet, it's all kids. I guess I'll know in time."

Let me tell you how awesome God is & how awesome faith is. I met my husband within months after asking God, "Was my future husband in my wallet?" After dating my husband a few months, he noticed one of the pictures in my wallet looked familiar. He then revealed to me that he was Santa @ the Beverly Hills Mall the previous Christmas & the Santa in the picture with the children I had nannied, was him. I looked @ the picture again and guess what? It was indeed him! My husband! He even remembered there were two nannies, a Spanish girl and a caucasian girl. He said, "I didn't see you." I said, "It was my day off, so I wasn't there." God had answered a big prayer of mine months ago and I didn't even know, as my father often says, "it was already done.

I learned to pray specifically and I learned to break it down. In my book, I talk about how God granted me the husband I defined to him

& trust me, I had my checklist. God granted me the desires of my heart. I would check my list off as our relationship grew. Once the last check was made, I knew he was indeed, God appointed. (PBF CH 11, Pg 68-70)

Psalm 20: 1-9 (NIV)

1. May the Lord answer you when you are in distress; may the name of the God of Jacob protect you.

2. May he send you help from the sanctuary and grant you support from Zion.

3. May he remember all your sacrifices and accept your burnt offerings.

4. May he give you the desire of your heart and make all your plans succeed.

5. May we shout for joy over your victory and lift up our banners in the name of our God. May the Lord grant all your requests.
6. Now this I know: The Lord gives victory to his anointed. He answers him from his heavenly sanctuary with the victorious power of his right hand.

7. Some trust in chariots and some in horses, but we trust in the name of the Lord our God.

8. They are brought to their knees and fall, but we rise up and stand firm.

9. Lord, give victory to the king! Answer us when we call!

Now Imagine yourself, sitting in your place of prayer, looking to the heavens & talking with our Lord & Savior, Jesus Christ. You are praying & declaring to him the desires of your heart. Define your desires. Be specific. BREAK IT DOWN! Name something of faith, that you don't have, that you see God already giving you? If it is HIS will, He WILL design it for You & You alone.

We all want to feel like we are ready for all God's blessings, though God knows when its time. Sometimes it take years to get your prayer answered, then you look back & realize why you had to wait it out. Let me give you an example of this. Throughout my marriage, when times got tough, I tried to leave my husband 4 times.

One time, it worked temporarily, though 3 times it failed completely. God would not allow it. Every time it fell through. I used to scream, "Lord please, let me go! I'm trying to raise Godly children in what I sometimes felt was an ungodly marriage. Please let me go!"

In the last chapters of my book, "Pure Blind Faith," I talk about our challenges. (PBF Ch 15, Pg 114-130) My father always said, "When God was working on Moses, he was hardening Pharaoh's heart." What does that mean?, I thought. Later I learned the meaning, that Pharaoh heart was hardened because the death of his son He realized that Moses God was God and freed the .slaves That saying puzzled me until the weekend my husband & I's life changed forever.(PBF Ch 16, Pg 131-143)

I then understood what my father was saying to me all along. God was working with babe and I, both of us at the same time.. We've been happily married now for 19 years and at perfect peace together. As the gospel artist, Andrae Crouch sings." I will keep you perfect peace you keep your mind stayed on ME." (Perfect Peace…you can find it on YouTube)

What is the desire of your heart? Are you prepared for that desire? What will keep you in Perfect Peace?

Chapter Twelve
GOD'S TIMING!

HIS plan is so much better than ours.

Hebrew 11 (NIV)
Faith in Action

1. Now faith is confidence in what we hope for and assurance about what we do not see.

2. This is what the ancients were commended for.

3. By faith we understand that the universe was formed at God's command, so that what is seen was not made out of what was visible.

4. By faith Abel brought God a better offering than Cain did. By faith he was commended as righteous, when God spoke well of his offerings. And by faith Abel still speaks, even though he is dead.

5. By faith Enoch was taken from this life, so that he did not experience death: "He could not be found, because God had taken him away. before he was taken, he was commended as one who pleased God.

6. And without faith it is impossible to please God, because anyone who comes to him must believe that he exists and that he rewards those who earnestly seek him.

7. By faith Noah, when warned about things not yet seen, in holy fear built an ark to save his family. By his faith he condemned the world and became heir of the righteousness that is in keeping with faith.

8. By faith Abraham, when called to go to a place he would later receive as his inheritance, obeyed and went, even though he did not know where he was going.

9. By faith he made his home in the promised land like a stranger in a foreign country; he lived in tents, as did Isaac and Jacob, who were heirs with him of the same promise.

10. For he was looking forward to the city with foundations, whose architect and builder is God.

11. And by faith even Sarah, who was past childbearing age, was enabled to bear children because she considered him faithful who had made the promise.

12. And so from this one man, and he as good as dead, came descendants as numerous as the stars in the sky and as countless as the sand on the seashore.

13. All these people were still living by faith when they died. They did not receive the things promised; they only saw them and welcomed them from a distance, admitting that they were foreigners and strangers on earth.

14. People who say such things show that they are looking for a country of their own.

15. If they had been thinking of the country they had left, they would have had opportunity to return.

16. Instead, they were longing for a better country, a heavenly one. Therefore God is not ashamed to be called their God, for he has prepared a city for them.

17. By faith Abraham, when God tested him, offered Isaac as a sacrifice. He who had embraced the promises was about to sacrifice his one and only son.

18. even though God had said to him, "It is through Isaac that your offspring will be reckoned." 19. Abraham reasoned that God could even raise the dead, and so in a manner of speaking he did receive Isaac back from death.

20. By faith Isaac blessed Jacob and Esau in regard to their future.

21. By faith Jacob, when he was dying, blessed each of Joseph's sons, and worshipped as he leaned on the top of his staff.

22. By faith Joseph, when his end was near, spoke about the exodus of the Israelites from

Egypt and gave instructions concerning the burial of his bones.

23. By faith Moses' parents hid him for three months after he was born, because they saw he was no ordinary child, and they were not afraid of the king's edict.

24. By faith Moses, when he had grown up, refused to be known as the son of Pharaoh's daughter.

25. He chose to be mistreated along with the people of God rather than to enjoy the fleeting pleasures of sin.

26. He regarded disgrace for the sake of Christ as of greater value than the treasures of Egypt, because he was looking ahead to his reward.

27. By faith he left Egypt, not fearing the king's anger; he persevered because he saw him who is invisible.

28. By faith he kept the Passover and the application of blood, so that the destroyer of the firstborn would not touch the firstborn of Israel.

29. By faith the people passed through the Red Sea as on dry land; but when the Egyptians tried to do so, they were drowned.

30. By faith the walls of Jericho fell, after the army had marched around them for seven days.

31. By faith the prostitute Rahab, because she welcomed the spies, was not killed with those who were disobedient.

32. And what more shall I say? I do not have time to tell about Gideon, Barak, Samson and Jephthah, about David and Samuel and the prophets,

33. Who through faith conquered kingdoms, administered justice, and gained what was promised; who shut the mouths of lions,

34. Quenched the fury of the flames, and escaped the edge of the sword; whose weakness was turned to strength; and who became powerful in battle and routed foreign armies.

35. Women received back their dead, raised to life again. There were others who were tortured, refusing to be released so that they might gain an even better resurrection.

36. Some faced jeers and flogging, and even chains and imprisonment.

37. They were put to death by stoning; they were sawed in two; they were killed by the sword. They went about in sheepskins and goatskins, destitute, persecuted and mistreated.

38. The world was not worthy of them. They wandered in deserts and mountains, living in caves and in holes in the ground.

39. These were all commended for their faith, yet none of them received what had been promised.

40. Since God had planned something better for us so that only together with us would they be made perfect.

God timing is always the right timing. Don't get impatience, antsy, agitated or restless. He hears your prayers and will answer it in his timing. You can be homeless, sleeping in your car thinking God doesn't hear you but God maybe preparing you for the next chapter in your life.

Think, think, think about it????

"For if I never had a problem, I wouldn't know that God could solve them, I'd never know what **FAITH** in GOD could do."

From the song "Through It All"
          By Andrae Crouch

YouTube It.

Chapter Thirteen
Remember what GOD said:

"If you have faith as small as a mustard seed, you can say to this mulberry tree, 'Be uprooted and planted in the sea,' and it will obey you.

Luke 17:6 (NuIV)

On a personal note:

Today is January 14, 2020. I am finishing this guidebook with blood in my eyes from diabetes. Everything is blurry and doubled but I am determined to finish this guidebook and start a new one "The Art of Love". My PBF prayer is by the end of 2020 this will be long forgotten and my vision will be normal. I wanted to share my latest faith based prayer with you all, so you can see the power of faith and prayer.

Are you now ready for your special gift of FAITH? Let's start practicing it.

What will be your first acts of faith?

When did God answer it? Write down the journey of the answered prayer.

NOTES

NOTES

NOTES

www.ingramcontent.com/pod-product-compliance
Lightning Source LLC
Chambersburg PA
CBHW081637040426
42449CB00014B/3356